Six Figure Speaker

How To Create a Six Business by Sharing Your Passion

★ ★ ★ ★ ★
TURNING PASSION
INTO PROFITS

SCAN ME

Printed and bound in Great Britain by Clays Ltd, Elcograf S.p.A.

Legal Notice

The information presented herein represents the views of the author as of the date of publication only, due to rate with which conditions and procedures change the author reserves the right to alter and update his opinion on such matters as necessary. This book is for information purposes only and whilst every attempt has been made to verify the information provided, neither the author nor any affiliates/partners assume any responsibility for errors, inaccuracies or omissions. Any slights or people or organisations are unintentional. You should be aware of any laws which govern business transactions or other business practises in your country or state and adhere to the relevant laws. Any reference to any person, business or organisation whether living or dead is purely coincidental.

Every effort has been made to represent this product and its potential accurately. Examples shared in this booker not to be interpreted as a promise or guarantee and are used as a real life example. The earning potential is entirely based on the person using the product and no promise or guarantee is offered nor given for such results. This is not a get rich quick scheme and all claims made by the author can be verified. Your level of success in attaining results claimed in our material is very much dependant on various factors such as but not limited to your dedication, time spent, financial situation, knowledge and implementation. We do not make any guarantees of success or otherwise, nor are we responsible for your actions as a result of reading this book.

Any and all forward looking statements here or on any of our sales material are intended to express our opinion of earning potential. Many factors will be important in determining your actual results an no guarantee will be provided.

No part of this book may be reproduced in part or full without written permission from the copyright holder namely Alasdair Cunningham, this is to include but not limited to digital, photocopying, screenshots or hard copy

Contents

Chapter 1

What it means to be a Speaker?

Think of all the great speakers you can and ask yourself what do they all have in common? Go ahead and list them below

-
-
-
-
-
-
-
-

In my opinion they all have some common traits and that's what makes them stand out from the rest and I'm sure you wrote down many of the same values and skills above that I believe all great speakers have in common, namely high integrity, power, presence, honesty, respect, decisiveness, great communicators, gratitude, empathy, sympathy, ability to influence, courageous, self awareness, responsibility, accountability and ownership, I truly believe that great speakers are also great leaders and I also believe that the skill to becoming a great speaker can be a learned skill. I know this because that's exactly what I did when I took the decision to learn how to master the stage, what happened was that;

- I grew in confidence to a level that I never imagined possible
- I changed my habits to change my mind patterns
- I developed a mindset so strong that nothing would ever get in my way

- I became a world class authority and speaker
- I helped thousands of people to change their mindset and lives
- I lead teams to grow and thrive in any economy
- I attracted people into my world, new clients, now contracts and business opportunity

For me becoming a speaker became a passion of mine and therefore is a non-negotiable, as I believe you're either leading, following or standing still so you must choose where you're at. I chose to speak and lead.

For some the mere thought of leading a team scares them. For me the thought of following or being stagnant scares me so I opted for the leading role in as many aspects of my life as I could. That doesn't mean I lead every aspect, a good leader knows when they have to adapt to a following role and with every aspect I assess what's best for the role and then I adopt the relevant position.

Before we get started let me introduce myself and tell you a little about myself so you know what I'm all about, My name is Alasdair Cunningham and the person I am today couldn't be further from the person I grew up as, in the sense of I was someone that would completely shy away from any sort of attention or limelight. I grew up in a small village in rural Scotland and we tend to be pretty shy and quiet people.

During school and early years education I would literally avoid any sort of group activity, tend to keep myself to myself and do literally anything to avoid any sort of interaction with people. I used to blush brighter than a tomato with any sort of attention and I struggled throughout most of my life with this and it was always there with me and restricted literally everything I done whether that be social, personal and business.

Working my way through school, college and starting off in my career this whole phobia of blushing and shying away from any sort of limelight always held me back. This issue was always there and although I couldn't quantity or financially value it, it definitely has lost me many opportunities and business growth.

As I look back over my life I can pin point multiple occasions where I took myself out of the game because of not wanting to put myself forward, make myself heard, or step up and take control. I very much took a back seat and just went along with it. This happened personally and in business and honestly knowing what I know now I laugh and cringe at myself about how I used to be.

After leaving education I went through an apprenticeship and trained on commercial vehicle engineering which led me to working amongst large teams of mainly older aged men who had been in the industry for many years. As an apprentice in a working class industrial type job you'd better be expecting to have the piss ripped out of you and honestly be put through some "initiation" type team building experiences. All I'll say is if apprentices today had to go through the "team building exercises" that apprentices back in the day did then there would an awful lot of health and safety claims, complaints and hurt feelings!

I know for sure HR department would be busy as hell dealing with the repercussions of said experiences.

Unfortunately we do live in a little bit of a snowflake age just now, as offensive as that may seem it's very much evident. I actually think the way I was trained through my apprenticeship taught me to become the person I am today and honestly I wouldn't have it any other way.

Let me give you an example of one of the "experiences" my peers "forced" (and I say forced very loosely) me do. I was working within a bus and coach team with around 25 other engineers and every day it was the apprentices job to make the drinks for all the engineers, sounds easy I know but here's the thing, we had to make everyone's drink from memory without a list, and believe me not all but certainly the foreman and main ring leaders were very particular about there preferred drink, for example Andy, our foreman had coffee with 3 sugars, 3 heaped teaspoons of coffee, no milk and it must be in a particular cup. Sounds easy but now add that to everyone's else's order and factor in the time limit of just 8 minutes to make everyones drinks, if we're late or any orders were wrong or even tasted slightly wrong then there was consequences. On one occasion when I messed it up the consequence was that I had to entertain the whole team over the tea break by either singing the latest radio hit's or by doing stand up comedy for the whole tea break. You had a choice here to either comply or not and let me tell you, you chose to comply. Non compliance here takes the consequences to the next level.

Needless to say, I learnt a lot during these days, I learnt how to build teams, have fun within the teams, give and receive banter and most importantly build relationships with people of all levels and backgrounds. Although it sounds distressing it really wasn't, it was actually fun and very good for us although it did now and again get out of hand momentarily.

No one ever got hurt, maybe a few got a little embarrassed, myself included but ultimately its was all fun to help pass the days at work. Some of the best relationship skills came from these experiences. Although I enjoyed the workshop scene I knew deep down that I wanted more so after years of service and running various businesses in the industry I made the toughest decision of my life which at the time petrified me as

I was leaving behind everything I knew and had worked for to venturing into a world of unknown.

I was already an amateur investor in buy to let property so decided to step into this sector and fully commit and that meant educating myself, I won't go into too much detail here about what I have achieved in property as you can read all about my property business in my book "Whatever It Takes", in a nutshell my business in property went very well and I found my self in a position of financial freedom and having time on my hands as my passive income was working very well for me.

The thing is everyone wants time, but when you have lots of time the novelty soon wears off and I actually started to become very unhappy and down, and honestly this whole financially free and having time on my hands was not all it cracked up to be. Now I have time, what can I do with it? I'll cover how I ended up becoming an accidental speaker in the next chapter but for now, i'll tell you that I forced myself into personal development by starting to push myself outside of my comfort zone and as a result I've experienced massive results, achievements and gratitude that I never knew possible and it's all because I understood the principle of serve before you sell and first you must learn and become a bigger person before you can help others.

Today, I've helped many people and have inspired many of them change their perspective, mindset and future by gaining the skills to become great leader, investor, and entrepreneur in their chosen path. One of the greatest pleasures I get in my life is truly seeing others have some sort of "click" and what I mean by that is that they have that moment in life where they realise that they can actually do this. I believe every person irrespective of who, what or where they have come from has the inner ability to rise and shine above and be their best success story, Success is very much an individual milestone and is measured very differently by each person, some measure success by their bank balance where by others measure by their happiness

Here's just a few of the many messages I get from people after spending we have worked together;

Couldn't thank you enough for the amazing day, a real me came forward and like you told me 2 months ago, it has been a really powerful to see it happened. You are an amazing man, and thanks for what you do that so many of us, if not all, will become THE VOICE. Have a good night Alasdair. 23:57

18/05/2021

Hey Alasdair,
I'm really looking forward to seeing you all next week at LOB!!
Some of us from TTW had a great catch up on Thursday, reflecting and supporting each other- I've been thinking about your impact on people and the way you build communities and it's absolutely amazing. We are all in a better place and are grateful- thank you!! Have a nice day 😊 😊 12:31

Hi Alasadair, I just want to thank you for everything that you are doing! The impact you have had on my life has been massive! I was just going over my feedback notes from tell the world and thought of you. I'm very optimistic about what the future holds for me and wanted to share that with you. You are a very solid guy and I appreciate the time and effort you have invested into all our lives. Hope you're enjoying you bank holiday. 🍻 16:10

Mate it's honestly no bother,. Thanks for the message tho it's appreciated 22:04

Hey Alasdair, It's Alex here sure you have received lots of messages today. I would just like to thank you from the bottom of my heart. You are a wonderful man and I appreciate everything you, Ricci and the rest of the Samuel Leeds training group have done for me and Annalisa. You are changing lives. Words can't describe how I feel but Thankyou for the past few days it's been amazing and I will look forward to meeting you again. Take care and all the best 😊 18:48

These are just a few messages I have received from delegates after they heard me speak and we have worked together at events.

Being in a position to empower and inspire people is a truly amazing place to be. I believe I was meant to train and inspire and watching each and every person I work with grow and develop is what it's all about for me. I believe everyone has a message to share and your community needs you to share it, I know that me sharing my message has saved lives and I know me training others to speak they have also gone on to save lives. I trained a ex military service man how to present and deliver a message and after the event he then went onto to share his message on instagram and other sites, and as a direct result of his message, a fellow service man reached out to him to ask for help.

Now, he didn't know this person apart from a common interest in social media but the message was delivered in such a powerful way that this person felt ok to reach out and ask for help, you see it's about who you can help and provide hope for and that's why you all need to become speakers because speakers lead the way and show others who are not quite where you're at that's it ok and that they to can become leaders.

I believe leaders create more leaders not followers but we live in a world where the leaders we see on social media are superficial and quite frankly more interested in how they look and are perceived than helping people and it's been proven many times.

How about we all stand tall and create a generation of true leaders and for me the only way to do that is to become a world class speaker where you share your message to the masses with integrity, honesty and care, and that exactly why I chose to write this book.

So Lets crack on and make this happen

Chapter 2

Accidental Speaker

I'm sure you've all met someone who you perceive is a natural leader, a person that naturally attracts people and business, the sort of person that no matter what happens they are head strong, stand loud and proud and pave the way for others to follow, we have all seen them and I'm sure your reading this with someone in mind. It seem's that no matter what they turn their hands to it turns to gold. Some people just have that natural leadership flare in everything they do, they do everything with a hint of ease and they seem to take everything in their stride where nothing phases them, nothing gets to them and they just seem to get things done and make stuff happen. Often they exude social dominance and have the gift of being thrown into any situation and coming out on top. I know you know what I'm talking about and I know you have someone in mind that fits that bill.

As I grew up I watched others around me thrive in these situations I would always kinda be thankful that the limelight wasn't on me, you see I was not a naturally gifted and confident person, I didn't have the personality, attitude, confidence or mindset to be in the limelight as is I grew up as a very shy and quiet person, someone who would avoid confrontation, social scenes and any sort of attention, quite literally if I got any attention I used to feel myself blushing and getting more and more embarrassed. I would just want to curl up into a little ball until the situation passed, and this resulted in me avoiding all social scenes, parties, trips out with friends, and even sports. I wouldn't do anything that meant people watched as I always had this fear of judgement, the fear that people are laughing at me or critiquing me and I hated every minute of it.

It's so ironic that I grew up like that yet today I have no issue at all standing speaking in front of 1000's of people without even thinking about it. The person I am today is far from the person I was even just a few years ago. I know that person you are does not dictate who you can become. It's a choice to change and today I hope you take the choice to become a leader and step up.

So how did I get from a negative shy person who literally couldn't do anything that meant attention to someone who presents to large audiences on a weekly basis, someone who has spoken at events literally every week across the country, in Europe and as far a field as India and Uganda.

Here's how it all started

As the title says I became an accidental speaker, in the sense of I never intended on ever being a speaker. It happened because I became super successful in the field of property and I was then asked to share my success at various property events, these events ranged from networking events with half a dozen people to several hundred people at seminars and this started with me being asked to jumped on stage and answer a few questions, provide a testimonial to in time running main events and training others to do the same.

The first time I ever took to a stage was at a hotel in Victoria, just opposite Victoria coach station and there was a room of around 80 people and Samuel asked me to share what I had been up to and how I had just secured my latest property deal.

Now, Samuel said to me before hand I may ask you to share. "Ok, cool no worries I replied" deep down I'm actually thinking you gotta be kidding. I am not going up there to talk, it will be a complete disaster, I've never done this before and

I'll just crumble and I'll end up mumbling my words, forgetting what I want to say, stutter and get all embarrassed, Everyone will laugh and I'll be the laughing stock of the event.

The reality is far different as the audience is very much understanding and forgiving and just want to learn as I found out, before I knew it Samuel had invited me on the stage and was handing me a microphone and before I know it he's firing questions at me, literally one after another and I'm losing track of what I'm saying, my palms are sweating and I can feel my nerves coming through my body, I remember having to put my hand in pocket to try and keep the shakes under control.

Literally this was the most intense awkwardness I've felt for a long time and I hated every minute of it. Although I was only on stage for a few minutes It felt like an hour. Samuel wrapped up, thanked me and the audience applauded me as I walk off the stage.

Great, I'm relieved it's over and honestly I'm not wanting to ever do that again. A few hours passed by and my nerves are calmed and I'm telling myself it wasn't that bad, I didn't do that bad I keep saying, After the event I was approached by a couple of delegates and they came to shake my hand and ask me questions. They were saying it was refreshing to hear real honest feedback about the industry and that they took a lot from what I said on stage. But, here's me thinking I sucked but clearly the audience took something from what I said so that made me feel a whole lot better. Ok maybe it's not so bad being on stage, I mean clearly I helped someone so that makes it worthwhile and bearable.

Over the course of the next few months I was invited to speak at more and more events, mostly consisting of short 5 to 15 minutes question and answer sessions but I was actually starting to enjoy the opportunities and was beginning to actually find it easier and easier to get on stage. I was still nervous but nowhere near as bad as I once was.

It's like anything, the more you do the better you get, and I was open to the opportunity to get on stage, speak to people as often as I could. Knowing that by sharing my success in property is helping others and that feeling of knowing that something I've said or done has inspired others to do is a feeling that is hard to replicate. As more and more events went by and more and more opportunities to speak came my way I went by the motto say yes and figure it out later, I know that to grow as a speaker I needed to take every opportunity put my way.

To start with all I was doing was question and answer sessions, I still at this point hadn't actually been alone on the stage, every time I'd taken to the stage I had support from the main speaker but I think it's about time I stood on my own and took control, doesn't seem like a big task but trust me it is.

Standing in a room being supported and led by the lead speaker is one thing, now I have to be the lead speaker and that is not a task to be frowned upon. This is next level so I took an opportunity to do just that, I was at an event with around 40 delegates and the lead speaker knowing I wanted to progress invited me to open the event and introduce him to the front. This takes around 5 minutes and would involve me welcoming the delegates and giving a brief overview of what they can expect from the day followed by a little biography of the main speaker and then introducing him to the stage.   This is one of the most important parts of any event as it sets the context and expectations fo the event.

Simple! Right.

Well, this was the worst experience of my life and I still have nightmares about it today. Literally all my childhood fears and worries came flooding back, a complete disaster and honestly the worst experience of my life. Here's what happened;

The audience is excited and chatting amongst themselves getting to know each other, I walk up the front and stand front and centre awaiting for them to quiet down, this takes what seems like minutes. As they calmed and are all eyes forward I started....

What should I be saying here? My mind has gone completely blank. I'm trying my best to remember what I was told to say but for the life of me I couldn't get it from my head out of my mouth and I just stood there looking blank, eventually after an age, I managed to get a few words out which were nothing like what I was supposed to be saying, it went something like this

Hello, and welcome. You're all in for a treat today but before we get started let's find out where you're all from?

I then spent the next few minutes asking people where they were from. What the heck is going on? This is not to script! Why do I care where they're from? What difference does it make? The reasons I asked is because I once heard a speaker ask the audience where they had travelled from so I went with that but what happened was the audience and myself became very awkward and honestly I just wanted to be swallowed whole by the ground at this point.

As I continued to introduce the speaker, I started to talk about Samuel, I could hear myself repeating myself line by line and I think I said about five times that he's a great guy, honestly he's a great guy I kept saying over and over.

I need to get myself out of here as soon as possible, I skipped the rest of my opening and I moved onto the intro

"Ladies and gents please welcome your lead trainer Mr Samuel Leeds" and out came Samuel to the room

Wait actually no he didn't, you see Samuel and his brother Russell had just listened to my shameful introduction from the back room and were busy laughing their heads off that they didn't hear me introduce Samuel so Samuel didn't come out and I had to shout him again.

I am not doing this again that's for sure, Samuel graced the stage and took over and the event went off like a bomb and was amazing to watch. On our debrief Samuel gave me a bit of stick but he finished by saying this

"Every master was once a disaster" and that's stuck with me ever since. Thankfully I never gave up and I kept going back and learning to speak on stage. Good job I did as I would need the skill to speak in front of a large audience sooner than expected.

I was invited out Africa to assist on some charity work with Samuel and his team and this was looking to be a great experience however I was a little apprehensive about going. The week was to be a tough week as we were visiting areas that Samuel had previously visited to install fresh water tanks and then we were planning on visiting new potential sites for the next installations, we were also holding a business conference in Jinja which was organised by our local guide. We're expecting a reasonable turnout of around 200 as they have been advertising on local radio stations for several weeks now.

Before the week commenced we decided to have a day of team building which was originally supposed to be all of us going bungee jumping over the Victoria River, however there was an issue on the day with the company organising the jump so we couldn't take part so we opted to go white water rafting. I've done this several times before and we're all pretty excited about it, we had to get up river so we set out on the two hour bus trip to the start point which to us north of Jinja. As we all jumped on board it kinda felt that there were too many of us in the raft, anyway we set off in to the waters.

The waters were clam and relaxing, smooth soft waters as we drift slowly down river, I remember watching kids playing on the banks whilst just reflecting on life and enjoying the peaceful moments watching the world go by. Soon the peace ended as we hit the first set of waterfalls, we were shouted some last second instructions from the guide, nerves and anticipation were high as we entered the falls, Here we go, Hold on and be ready, he shouted!

HARD LEFT - HARDER - BACK LEFT PADDLE it was just loads of shouting and honestly I remember very little about this part apart from the panic we were all experiencing. I like others lost my paddle in the waters and what followed took me years to get over.
We were hurtling though the waterfall which is a grade 5 falls and we were heading in nose first, the guide clearly said before hand its is imperative we go in sideways not nose first yet here we were nose first. As we head down getting thrown all over the place the nose of the raft went not a whirlpool at the bottom, all I remember was seeing the sky, the raft had pitched up in the air and the rolled to the side, myself and 4 others were on the right hand side of the raft and this was the high side, all of us were thrown from the raft into the water.

What you must not forget is these waters are filled with boulders and rocks and I felt everyone on the way down river. Under the overturned raft is an air pocket which we were all told if the raft overturn, grab hold of the ropes on the raft and stay in the air gap, this is exactly what I done and let me tell you, there was no air gap. I couldn't get out from underneath the raft and it was keeping me under the water whilst being thrown into the rocks, There was no air, I was being pulled under the water and the safe zone under the raft was actually drowning me.

After what seemed like a long time I managed to free myself and found myself at the bottom of the waterfall, the trip down wasn't smooth by any means, numerous interactions with rocks on the way down left its toll on my body but I'm alive and appear to be in tact. I'm in the water with who knows what else and I try to regain some composure but I'm in panic mode, I'm drifting further and further away from any team members and I can't actually see the raft or even waterfall now as we went around a bend. I could hear screams and managed to see Anna, she was probably 100 metre away up river to my position, so I tried to swim to her to help her, she has two girls and I need to do what I can to help and make sure she's safe.

As I'm trying to swim back I simply can't, swimming up river is like running on a treadmill, you don't actually get very far and all that was happening was I was getting pulled further down river. Now, I drifting down the river uncontrollably and although it seems hell is breaking loose there was also an element of peace around, it was very quiet and the waters appeared calm on the surface. The water is extremely deceptive and dangerous and actually were pulling me down river.

I was screaming to Anna to get to the side and I was trying to get over to her to help her but in the background I could hear rushing water, a I looked behind me I see the white of water as it foams and heads over another water fall and I'm getting pulled straight to the scene, at this point I'm completely powerless and as I get closer the second waterfall I start getting pulled under water again.

I'm drowning! And that's how I'm going to die, alone in the River Nile on a trip that I never really wanted to be on. This cannot be happening, I remember getting pulled under the water a lot and it seemed I was under for minutes but in reality it was seconds. I was panicking and swallowing water and there came a point when I actually gave up and just lay there and accepted my fate.

Its funny because it's the one time in my life when I faced death and I truly believe that I faced death that day, what saved me? You see the whole time this was going on I was not thinking about anything other my family and my two girls, That's what saved me! I briefly saw what their life looked like without me around and that was what made me fight to survive.

There is no way I'm putting Lisa in a place where she has to tell my daughters that daddy is not coming home, so I fight and swim as hard as I can to stay afloat, and as I headed into the second waterfall I lay on my back and braced myself for a second run and thankfully this was one was not quite as bad as the first waterfall, Don't get me wrong the experience was not one I want to do again. Long story short I survived and made it out the other end.

As I came through the other side I managed to get myself to Anna, we're now holding onto each other awaiting help so we swim over to the banks to find security, some time went by and eventually a rescue raft appeared. This was one of the best things I've seen in a while and honestly the relief was immense. We climbed on board with the help of the crew and they then proceeded up river to where everyone else was, by this time we have been in the river for around 1 hour and had drifted around 500 yards down river. It took us a good

10 minutes to get back to our colleagues and both Anna and myself were hoping and praying everyone was ok.

As we arrived back on the banks I could see everyone was there, most have cuts, bruises and in severe pain. Our guide Charles is bleeding from his feet, it looks like he may need surgery on his toes as they appear to have been cut or ripped open, most of our colleagues were walking wounded and then there was Samuel, I could see him resting on the front of a raft and his leg was being supported.

As I got closer to him I could see the blood and see the pain in his face, Samuel had actually broken his leg and the bone was exposed, he was in severe pain and losing blood, the problem is we're in the middle of nowhere with no NHS, Ambulance or help anywhere nearby. We had to very quickly fix this problem so we called our taxi driver who met us and we climbed in his minivan, the back seats had 5 of our team squash in and on the front was Samuel laying across the seats with me supporting his leg and stopping him moving it. I literally remember him passing out several times and now his leg just wouldn't stop bleeding, we had wrapped his leg but that just slowed it, our priority now is to get everyone to hospital as soon as possible and so far we've been driving 1 hour and I'm not sure were anywhere near, all the driver kept saying was nearly there and he said this time and time again. It seemed like 2-3 hours before we arrived and on arrival we were met by the hospital staff who rushed Samuel into a room. Everyone else was treated and apart from Samuel as we're all walking wounded to varying levels but by far Samuel's the one is serious bother here.

The facts are this were in the middle of Jinja, in a third world country in a hospital in the middle of a shanty town with no English speaking doctors. Samuel isn't going anywhere and we're all in pretty bad shape. Several hours pass by and finally a doctor comes out to say Samuel needs surgery and needs it straight away. We finally get an opportunity to check in on our friend.

This was when I realised Samuel real grit and mission driven passion, Samuel was laying in bed, all of us around him and he basically took control of the whole situation, even though he was drugged up and in severe pain he led a briefing of what we're going to do,

Samuel Says

"Right, it's happened but our pain is temporary, the reason we're here is to fix their pain so we have a choice, we can all go home or those who can physically continue should continue with the mission, now I'm not going anywhere for several days probably weeks but you can continue in my shoes"

As much as I really wanted to pack up and fly home I knew we had to continue. There was no option here. Mission goes on.

Myself and Russell were tasked with being in charge and ensuring we fulfilled the trip and finished what we set out to do, Samuel said

"Alasdair, you need to step up and run the business workshop.
Russell, you need to find new sites and make sure our funds are spent as best as they can be"

Of course we obliged to Samuel's request and a few hours later we headed off to the hotel and left Samuel on his own, this was incredibly hard having to leave a team mate behind, but we knew he was super strong and we also had a few contacts coming to the hospital to be with him and ensure he was ok.

So we cracked on with the trip as per his wishes, and this started by us visiting the villages he had previously visited and supported, The village was great, we played football as best we could, we had fun, sat with the locals and had a few beers and saw the results of the water tanks that Samuel had installed a few years ago.

The next day was the business workshop, a conference room in Jinja with 200 seats laid out and I'm running it. I'm the lead speaker at this event yet I've never run an event before nor been on stage for more than 5 minutes unaccompanied. I was getting more and more comfortable on stage however to throw me in the deep end of having to run my own event in front of 200 in a foreign country where English is not widely spoken is going to be difficult to say the least.

It'll be fine I tell my self, I have the support of Russell, Stuart and John and between us I'm confident we'll deliver a great presentation. So I crack on and just get on with it. Like most things in life the more you worry about it the worse you play it out in your head so I decided let's just crack on and see what happens. What's the worst that could happen?

So I started, and before I know it the audience are engaging, getting involved and actually I feel finding the whole presentation very useful. Today we're teaching basic business, marketing and advertising as most are trying to start a little business for themselves.

We worked our way through the day and at the end we taught them how to prepare a simple business plan then they could present a plan to us in return for some investment from us for their new business ventures. A bit like dragons den style presenting, We invested around £5000 that day to 6 different entrepreneurs which you may think isn't a lot of money but in Uganda that money will go very far.

Over all the event was a success and I loved it, I think I'm finding my passion and it's really not what I ever thought it would be. I'm feeling a great sense pf pride that I've helped a local community create new businesses that will support themselves and other families. I'm still in contact with some of them today and after the event I got several messages from delegates on facebook to thank me for my time and teachings. The sense of pride when this happens is very high and it's a great feeling.

This was the start of me really wanting to push my speaking opportunities and I decided there and then that I would do whatever it takes to further that opportunity so that I can feel that pleasure of helping others. I then invested tens of thousands of pounds in training, mentoring with some of the world's best guru's travelling around the world taking every opportunity I could to speak on stage, learn from the best and implement my speaking ability.

Today, I've spoken at hundreds of events across Europe and further and inspired and help thousands of people to change their lives and mindset and grow their businesses through investing and business. So you see I never set out to be a speaker, in fact I owe it to Samuel breaking his leg that I got the bug to speak.

The reason I know you can also achieve what I have quite simply is because I did and I'm nothing special, I just got trained and then implemented like crazy by taking every opportunity that came my way. You'll feel the buzz I feel when you step on stage and see people's lives being changed as a direct result of something you have shared on stage and I truly believe that with the after effect of COVID 19 yet to be seen the world needs more trainers, speakers and leaders so it's your obligation that if you have a message that others need to hear then you must take the opportunities and tell the world about it and that's why I created a system to break it down for you and make it as simple as possible.

Let me guide through the 7 step process that I created called the Six Figure Speaker System.

Creating an easy to follow system has allowed me to train and mentor others to be able to prepare a 30 to 40 minutes presentation from scratch and deliver it in a way that people actually pay attention and remember what you spoke about.

I'll cover each segment over the course of this book and I know that if you follow the steps just like many others have you will by the end be able to put together a 30 to 45 minutes presentation on a subject you know, love and are passionate about

Let's get started.

Chapter 3

Speaker - Selecting your Topic

What topic should you choose to speak about? This is crucial because you want to ensure that what you speak about is firstly needed and secondly a topic that you're passionate about. Over this chapter I'll show you how to analyse what your potential audience want to hear about and how you can tailor your topic to suit your audience.

When I started on stage I initially shared my success in property and basically shared everything I've done to get where I have got to. You see selecting your topic is crucially important because you as a speaker are a bridge for your audience.

What I mean by this is you're the success story, you're the person that can bridge the gap between where they are now and where they want to be, you as a speaker can lead the way and show them how you achieved it, got there, fixed your issues and how you became the person you are today.

For instance, let's say you want to present about weight loss. Ask yourself do you have credibility in losing weight that can be verified? If the answer is yes then ask yourself, can you help other people looking to lose weight become healthier and happier and follow in your foot steps?

If you believe you can then you are the bridge between their unhappiness (A) and their end goal (B)

Your job is effectively take them from point A where they are right now to point B which is where the want to be. Now if you've done that successfully then you are more then qualified to help them get there. Now let's look at the other side of this and this is one of the problems I see with social media nowadays in that they're coaches, mentors and trainers out there offering training when they clearly know very little about the subject they are coaching and this is the problem. We have way to many fake teachers who are not or have never walked the walk within what they are speaking about.

One thing I am very serious about is the fact that I will prove everything I say I have done and if that means I whip out bank statements to prove earning claims, or documentation to prove ownership of property then so be it, I'll happily do this to any paying client.

I mean take the example above, if you were teaching weight loss but you're fat then the message you're sending out lacks integrity and you clearly don't follow your own teachings so why the heck should someone pay to hear what you have to say.

My point is only teach a topic that you class yourself as an expert in and understand the topic inside out. A subject you could talk about all day without notes and without having to research, You see the way I teach you to speak is to focus on the delivery and not on the content of the topic so for this to work you must know your topic inside out.

Take my topics, I teach several subjects, property, personal development, how to speak, how to present, facilitation, content creation and many more and every one of them I could with a moments notice be thrown on stage and deliver 1 hour of great value content and the reason for this is I know my topic through and through.

A great way to come up with your topic is to list every topic you know inside out. Let's do that now

-
-
-
-

Now we need to understand who actually wants to hear about that topic and a great way to do this is to search your topic on google and see what comes up. The idea is you want be as niche as possible and become the authority in that niche, for instance let's take the topic of a student of mine from a previous Tell The World program I ran in November last year.

The student is Danny and he is a car salesman, has been for 20 plus years and wanted to find a way to capitalise on his knowledge within the car sales industry. Danny was approached by many people looking to get into car sales as it can be quite a lucrative industry if done correctly so he put together a 1 day training event for those looking too fast track their way to making money from buying and selling cars. This is super niche and makes your topic way more valuable.

Let's check out a subject and do some research on this subject so for this exercise we can use the topic of Health and wellbeing, a very popular subject.

If you do some analysis on health and wellbeing the results that come back are very extensive and have been searched for

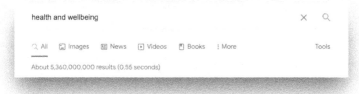

You can see that over 5.36 billion results come back from that search. How on earth are you ever going to get spotted amongst that search. The reality is you're never going to be found in this subject because other companies will be spending millions getting themselves seen.

So lets' try and be more niche, and more definitive on our subject and see how that effects the results, The more niche you can be the more targeted you can be with your marketing, advertising and planning on how you deliver your message.

health and wellbeing for over 40s						× Q
Q All	Images	Shopping	News	Videos	More	Tools

About 844,000 results (0.52 seconds)

See how almost instantly the amount of results that return when you add over 40's to the search criteria drops drastically to less than a million results. You will have a much better chance of getting spotted in this sector than just health and wellbeing so I would then make my topic around health and wellbeing for the over 40's.

Now if you're subject is health and wellbeing then I imagine, I mean I'm no expert but I imagine the principles of health and wellbeing are the same for all ages so why not target the over 40's in with your teachings, this serves several purposes, firstly, your advertising and marketing efforts will be considerably easier, the costs for marketing and advertising will be considerably cheaper as you're targeting a niche audience and secondly the over 40's will generally be more stable financially and most probably searching health and wellbeing for a reason! I know as someone hitting their 40's I can tell you my body is doing things it has never done before so I'm your ideal candidate!

The thing is people in their 40's will be more likely to be able to afford and more likely to value what you would offer and will see the value in what you bring therefore more inclined to be happy to pay for your coaching, mentoring or service.

You see how we've taken a very flooded market and broken it down to a much smaller market that you could easily dominate once you learn the skills of delivering your presentation to the market.

You can do this with any topic, The great thing for us is that people are always wanting to learn new skills and ways of doing things and they are always searching for someone to help them do that. I'm going to say again and again your job is to position your self in front of that person and make sure you are an expert that can deliver unique content in a way that stands out. Your job is to focus on the content delivery not the content as you should know the content.

The problem I see with many presenters is they are quite frankly boring on stage, this means that people don't relate to them and get bored watching them so they will never benefit from the presentation. If you focus a lot of effort on delivering the content exceptionally well and in a way that engaging and entertaining the client will receive the content better and retain more of it therefore more likely to actually use the content and implement it to get the results.

Remember this at all times

"Context over Content"

Now you need to choose your topic and find the niche that suits your expertise level, do your research and play around with the topic to find a topic subject that has a good amount of search results but not to few that means you can't make any money from it.

I would never target a topic that returns fewer than 100,000 results as this area will just be too difficult to work within and the demand is frankly just to low, You need to know that the marketing and branding you're planning will bring the rewards for your efforts and you don't want to waste too much time and effort targeting a market that is to small.
Remember there is nothing wrong with getting paid for your service or presentation because you're providing a solution to people problems and I've always gone by the ethos that when you help others get what they want then you will be rewarded accordingly. I've become a six figure speaker by doing exactly that and I truly believe I'm worth every penny I've learnt from serving people because I do this from a place of serve and help so rightly so if I've helped and served I should like you be getting paid for doing so.

So I need you before we head over to the next chapter to pin point your topic and do some research on this topic to try to carve out your niche within the market place for this topic

Go ahead - Write down your topic and let's move on to the next chapter

---

Chapter 4

Position Yourself As The Authority

If you're going to stand out in the industry you must position your self within that industry as an authority figure, You see the people who are often best known within a sector are not always the best at what they do but more often the best known, I'm positive that there are more successful property investors than myself yet I'm well known within the industry and seen as an authority by many, the 100's of messages I get tell me this, the fact that people come to see me speak tell me this and the fact that I get requested literally daily by people offering me money to spend time with me tells me this. They see me as an authority figure and as a result business comes my way along with business opportunities, joint ventures, finance and many other opportunities.

There are lots of way to help position you as an authority, think about it. What do your potential customer want from your business or by knowing or interacting with you? They generally want knowledge, your product or service so how can we offer them something of value with high perceived valued but at a low cost to you whilst building your credibility in the meantime.

Here's a few ideas books, podcast, blog posts, articles, video's, social media lives, postings on social media and many more high value low cost giveaways, so let's look at how I've done this and let's see how you can replicate this for your chosen topic, as I've already mentioned I started my speaking career by speaking at events all based around property investing.

Podcast

Alongside my business partner Russell I founded the Property Investors Podcast, a topical light hearted podcast all based around property where myself and Russell talk all about property and our businesses, the whole show is meant to be like two friends having a chat at the pub after work, We never wanted it to be serious, just two guys having a laugh and discussing property

The podcast is available on Spotify, Apple Podcast, YouTube, iTunes and most other podcast player platforms. Take the image above, this is the YouTube platform where we put the video of the podcast online and this page has 4000 subscribers, all of the podcast are filmed and uploaded here and the view rate is fairly strong.

Now for the listener this is a great free resource for finding out information, staying connected and getting to know myself and Russell by tuning in every Wednesday evening. You can see here that we reach a large amount of potential clients by offering a free podcast and doing it consistently every week

(Data collected from audio boom)

You can see that we have reached a lot of people and that we have on many occasion had over 750 listens per day. That 750 people per day interested in out topic and tuning in to hear what we have to say. Podcast reach the masses very quickly and in their own time so very convenient for the user.

YouTube Channel

Here's another free resource for my potential clients, I have a YouTube channel where I upload videos of what I'm up to in business detailing properties I'm buying, bought and working on to show people that I actually walk the walk and don't like many others just talk about it.

I document purchases and show timelines off the progress providing invoices and full disclosure of problems and successes. This channel has 1500 subs, videos mostly get over 1000 views each and some have gone as high at 5000 and one even went to 28000 views. This is by no means the most successful youtube channel but it doesn't need to be. It brings people into my world and builds up trust and credibility with any potential clients.

Here's my best performing video on YouTube, has had 28000 views and I got many message of the back of this video, go and watch this video when you get a minute and see why it's got way more views than most of my videos.

I can telly the main reason is most probably because the thumbnail picture, it's very money orientated and any topic that suggests making money will attract a lot of views. You will see when you watch the video I actually do what the title says to do.

Heres' another with 2900 views, very good video with lots of interaction, this video details a deal I'm working on and show the detailed numbers of the deal, meeting with builder and  me formulating the deal to see if the deal actually will make me money and deciding whether I should proceed with the deal, Again this is a real life deal that I'm an open book about and the viewed love this sort of video because it is genuine deal that can be tracked and observed.

My question to you is how can you document your business and topic on YouTube to build your position as an authority?

Become an Author

I decided whilst I was in Africa on a charity trip to start writing my book, the reason was I was getting messaged every day from people wanting me to teach them and help them and they all tended to have similar questions so I decided instead of answering everyone individually with the same answers I'd put the answers in a book, I also really struggled with understanding the legalities of a certain strategy and put that in the book as well as everyone who speaks about legalities massively overcomplicated it to make them sound clever when in fact it is simple.

The book is available and published on Amazon, I do offer this book free of charge on my personal website to those who search me but I sell it on amazon for £10.99, of which I get around £4.00 per copy and in its first year of release this booked generated over £15,000 in direct sales for me, but this is nothing in comparison to what it has generated me as a speaker.

This book is a lead generator only, I am not even bothered if I make any money from it as I use it to build my brand, my position and my authority within the industry which it has done very well. The amount of business I've done off the back of writing this book is unreal and the book in itself contains helpful high quality information that has helped many people get started on their business. So although the purpose was to build brand and awareness I also want to inspire and help others with it which it has definitely done.

And for those who don't like reading I also have the book available on Audible for listening. Again another form of media I use to reach a larger audience.

Even this book you're reading right now is being used to build my brand, position and authority within the space of public speaking. You're reading it for that very reason. Thank you!

Now if you said to me a few years ago that I would become a best selling amazon author I would have laughed in your face and told you to behave but the reality is just that I've become an amazon best seller and with a product I created from scratch, and even when I was writing it I honestly never thought anyone would buy anything I had written, especially seen as I am not the strongest at spelling and writing so who would buy and read what I had to say.

Well, the answer to that question is over 20,000 people that's who. It does make me laugh as I have a few negative comments about my book complaining that there is a spelling or grammatical error and I honesty just laugh at these, I actually couldn't care less what these people write, My books have helped many more that the few who have criticised it for a little spelling error. My question to those people is how many people have you helped?

So ask yourself can you write a book about your topic?

There are many ways to build credibility within your industry and topic, you just need to think a little creatively and be prepared to put yourself out there and be vocal about what you do and can offer people.

Podcast, YouTube, Books are just a selection but don't forget you can utilise social media to build your brand and position by adding lots of value to people and their life. Again if you help someone achieve what they want then in turn your time will come.

You can author articles and blog posts and submit them to various sites for posting which will all add value to the end user and help them see you as an authority. Avoid buying following or likes on social media, this will only damage your brand and authority as it easily identified and will actually affect your credibility, social media sites will rank you in order of popularity so if you lets say buy 10,000 followers from someone, most of these followers are robots and fake accounts so although your account may show 10,000 followers but your posts will not have the interaction from the users.

For instance a page I follow has 382,000 followers and they claim to be an authority in book publishing however their posts rarely get above 20 likes. This is actually very damaging for their page as it actually ranks them lower and punished them for buying followers and if you ask me, its all fake and lacks integrity. Build your following by being real and genuine and this will take time, but trust me it is worth it as your interaction is considerably higher.

Write down what can you do for your business to position yourself as an authority figure?

Chapter 5

Expert - Be the Expert

No one is coming to hear you speak if they don't see you as an expert because let's face it the world is full of people who talk about the subject but only the best leaders actually can do. It's imperative that you're not only the expert in the chosen subject but that your audience know you're the expert and you're the person known for that specific subject.

So how do we go about this? Well, firstly let's look at your subject and what qualifies you to speak about this subject.

Write down your subject

_____

Now write down what qualifies you to speak about the subject.

-
-
-
-
-
-
-

Great, now let me give you some examples of being an expert. I'll use myself as an example, You're reading my book right now and this whole book is about being a six figure speaker.

So the first thing I would want to know, Is the author a six figure speaker himself? This is easily proven and the answer is 100% yes. I can provide proof of contract to anyone who wishes to see.

Secondly; as the book is about speaking does the author actually speak on stage or doe she just talk about it. Again the answer is yes and again easily proven.

So straight away we can categorise me as an expert in this field, I'll expand on my expertise just incase you're doubting it.

There is no other speaker in the UK to my knowledge and I'm happy to be corrected that speaks at the number of events I speak at. In the last 12 months prior to Covid restrictions I spoke at over 60 events ranging from 20 people to over 1000 at each event, I was literally speaking at multiple events a week and sometimes 6 or 7 days back to back and pretty much living in hotels for that year as I travelled the country for speaking engagements. So if nothing else I've gained a hell of a lot of experience in that time and there's pretty much nothing I've not seen on stage nor had to deal with.

So as far a public speaking goes I can back everything I say up and have a lot of experience and knowledge through actually doing it. So I am suitably qualified to then teach others how I did it and how to make six figures doing so and that's the reason why I put this book and a training program together for it. Alongside this book I also offer a free training program called six figure speaker summit where you can come along and learn from me personally how and why you need to become a speaker and in turn get paid very well for doing so.

So you can see I'm an expert in this field, but let's look at some of the subjects I teach outside of speaking and i'll use property for this. So let's take a course I run about property called "Buy Refurbish Refinance Master class" the program is about buying a house, refurbishing the property to increase the value then exiting the deal via a re-finance. It's a very complicated subject and a lot harder than it sounds as there are lots of complex moving parts that all need to align if you're to make any money from the deal.

So let's look at my expertise level when it comes to this topic.

- I've completed and been involved in around 30 of these deals both for myself and with other investors so have seen many from start to completion
- Have two current properties that are in progress as I write this book one of which was bought for £210,000 and valued post work at £400,000
- I've documented deals I've done on my YouTube channel for complete transparency

Just a little bit of credibility but do you think I'm suitably qualified to teach people who haven't done what I've done, to show them the pitfalls and teach them how to do it from my experience?

Of course I am, you see if I was trying to teach people with more knowledge and experience than me then I wouldn't be suitable for that task but I'm not trying to teach them. I teaching people who want to achieve what I've achieved and as I'm doing it right now then I am more than qualified to teach this topic.

Again another field I teach is personal development and positive growth. As you've read I went through various stages of feeling worthless and depression and I've managed to work my way through this quite successfully so again I'm suitably qualified to talk about my experiences and how I managed to work around my issues.

I don't care what your topic is but it is essential that you can prove you're an expert in the field, and this must be honest, don't make up credibility as your audience will know very quickly and you will lose all integrity and reputation overnight.

Part of being an expert means you have to get your audience to know you're an expert in the quickest way possible without having a showreel of credits as that would alienate a lot of people. We need our audience to want to watch and listen and take note so it's imperative that we do this in a manner that comes across as humble.

We would do this in the form of an ETR, which mean Earn The Right, basically what gives you the right to speak and teach that subject and we break this down into two parts
A good ETR is build up with 70/30 story and credibility, you use this part to firstly tell them a little bit about yourself and what you are doing currently, this is your opportunity to explain who you are and gain a little instant authority by saying what you are doing. Let me give you an example;

"As I mentioned my name Alasdair, and over the last few years I've become a world class trainer and public speaker, I've spoken to tens of thousands of people and helped many of those people change the mindset and understand that they have massive potential as long as they're prepared to reach out grab it and today I'm going to speak to you and show you exactly how I can help you in the same way"

Now out of context this looks random but when you place into our CAPTURE system it fits perfectly. This part above is the first part of the ETR. You then need to continue with your expert positioning story.

Your expert positioning story is the story of how you got where you are now but you must start at the beginning and relive the pain you were feeling that led you to look for a change,

For instance if you're speaking about weight loss you could tell the story of the turning point of you having enough of being overweight.

- What happened?
- How did you feel?
- What pain did you experience?
- Were you disgusted with yourself for letting your body get like this?
- Did you feel shame?

You get my point, you need to take your audience back to your pain point and take them on that journey with you. It's so important you do this right because this whole session is about building trust and showing them that you're a real person. I guarantee if you're presenting to a group of overweight people who are looking to make a change and you get on stage and show them by telling your story that you were once feeling the exact same as they probably are right now then you will inspire and help most of them because they will relate to you.

Your expert positioning story should start with your pains, make them feel how you felt at the time, take them with on the journey of weight loss that you undertook, explain the steps, the struggles and the holdbacks and keep it real, then as your start to see success you tell them how you now feel, what happened and how did you do it?

Now, depending on how long your presentation will be depends on how long you do an ETR for. For a 45 minutes presentation your ETR should be around 5 minutes long and it must end on a high.

The purpose of the story is to connect and relate to your audience so they start to know, like and trust you quicker. Remember however it is imperative that any stories you tell must be true, the only exception that I will allow any of my students to do is to change a name for reasons of privacy but other than that they must be entirely true.

Stories Sell Facts Tell

Remember you're always selling so make sure you use the power of story telling to ensure you're selling your prospect onto working with you, believing in you, trusting you, understanding you and much more. I am not just referring to selling as a profit in money terms, I refer to selling and selling and idea, belief or way of doing something. You may find that you need top sell your clients on your skill level as an expert or sell them on the idea that they can achieve whatever it is they set out to achieve. There are a lot of people out there who need your expertise but in themselves may not believe that they have what it takes to get there so you need to sell them on the belief that they can if they set their mind to it.

Now that you've seen some working examples of my expertise I want you to look again at your topic and also again at your expertise level. Be honest with yourself and if you need to up skill then do that and do it quick. Don't get left behind because of complacency or pride just do and make sure you're always on top of your game.

Write down your subject

_____

Now write down what qualifies you to speak about the subject.

-
-
-
-
-
-
-

Now write your expert position story and work on that so it is in present tense and people can relate to it, remember this needs to be a little personal with stories of where you were and what was going on and then how you got to where you're at now, mix it with real life lessons and examples.

Remember they have come to see you because you're the expert who can help them get from point A to Point B as fast as possible, you "the expert" are the bridge for the gap between point A to B and once you master the six figure speaker system and have attended tell the world you will get paid very well for being that bridge.

As a trainer you provide the services and training needed from A to B as effectively as possible and only if you've done it yourself.

A question I get asked a lot is how much experience or credibility fo you need to then teach others? My answer to this is quite simple, if you have been there and done it and can back this up and you have the skills to teach then who's to say you shouldn't be teaching, as I mentioned earlier I have substantial creditability in what I teach but that doesn't make me the best or most successful, therefore I would only teach people that I feel I can help.

If I went to train people who had way more experience or credibility than myself then were going to have problems so all I would say is along as you genuinely believe you can help someone then you crack on and teach, inspire and guide whoever you wish to help.

Chapter 6

Asset - Build Assets within your Business

This chapter is to show you the power of social proof and assets for your business, now I'm not talking houses or conventional assets, I'm talking about assets such as Photographs, testimonials, feedback, social proof, articles written about you and anything else that makes you look good in the eye of the public. A public speaker needs assets to back up what they offer and increase the public perception of them and its an important part of the process and business building.

Social proof is a psychological and social phenomenon wherein people copy the actions of others in an attempt to undertake behaviour in any given situation. The term was founded by Robert Cialdini in his 1984 book Influence, and the concept is also known as informational social influence.

The whole concept is based around the idea that what people see they believe and trust, hence if you inform your customers of your product or service and tell them how great it is they are likely to realise that you are biased to say that so perhaps are not the best person to advise, however if someone else says how great your product or service is then that makes it ok.

Commonly referred to a herd behaviour the social proof concept is very much go with the masses type behaviour and the effects can be drastic.

There are five types of social proof that are referred to and commonly used

Expert

Expert social proof is when an expert in your industry recommends your products or services or is associated with your brand. Examples: a Instagram shoutout by an expert or having an expert on your instagram chat.

Celebrity

Celebrity social proof is when a celebrity endorses your products. Examples: an Instagram post or tweet about your product by a celebrity or influencer.

Client

Client social proof is when your current clients recommend your products and services based on their experiences with your brand. Examples: praises on social media or positive ratings on review sites by current or past clients.

Followers

This type of social proof is when a large group of people is seen to be endorsing your brand. Examples: having thousands of customers or millions of followers on your social media profiles.

Whether this is something you're aware off or are hearing about this for the first time I guarantee you that you have had decisions you have made influenced in such a manner, the reason being is we a humans a naturally inquisitive and like to conform with the masses. The sort of behaviour you may experience is habits such as stopping buying before you check out the company online or for online reviews, checking things like their social media to check for interaction on their posts from their customers.

The reason why social proof is essential is because we as humans have this need to have our decisions validated by others and to ensure that what we see confirms our decisions so we don't waste time or money.

Social Proof works because of human nature and there are many forms of social proof, for instance any online platform can provide a base for the proof to thrive. An example of this would be measuring your company or brands popularity on sites like facebook and instagram, If I was to purchase from a company one of the first things I would do is check them out on socials and I would look at things such as there comments on their posts, If these comments were all raving reviews and great feedback with lots of different real accounts replying then I can be pretty certain that the company or product is a

good choice for me, however if the popularity or interaction is very low, slow or negative I would form another opinion which would alter my buying decision.

Another form of social proof would be public appraisal and feedback, this is super powerful for any brand, business or product as the reviewed is likely to have been a customer and can verify a genuine experience.

Google carried out survey and found that 85% of consumers will trust a review they read online by a genuine user as much as they would trust a personal recommendation, and furthermore would trust that online review more than the companies own marketing materials. You can see why

reviews are so crucial for your business, brand or product and why you must have amazing customer service to deal with any issue as the manifest.

Two main types of social proof reviews and testimonials and these are user reviews and user generated content about your product, service or brand.
Here's an example of some social proof that I've got as assets for my business and brand

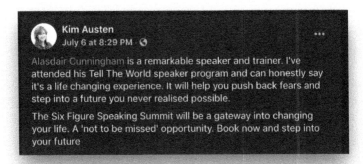

Here's a just two testimonials written by customers of mine who have used my services and heard me speak, they have taken it upon themselves to post on my page a testimonial about me and my brand. This type of user generated content is very powerful and I have literally hundreds of these messages. I advise that when they come through for you that you screen shot and save them on your computer for future use.

You should encourage users of your service or product to leave an honest review and feedback online for you. The more the better but do be aware that there will be occasion when you may not get the best review and this is to be expected as you can't always please everyone, as I've always been taught it's how you deal with any issues that makes your business so providing you deal with any complaints or negative review correctly then as far as I'm concerned it is what it is and I just deal with it and crack on with the business

Photographs of you doing what you do are a great way of building credibility and you absolutely should use the as assets for your business, I would use these pictures for marketing purposes as often as possible for several reasons.

Lets look at some examples of images I have as assets for my brand

Heres' a image of me on stage at our front end event the Property Investors Crash Course streamed virtually around the world, the reason why this is such a great asset is it shows me doing what I love and what I talk about and you can clearly see people in the back ground so it makes it real, obviously because it was a real event but in the eye of the viewer the image of the people in background speaks volumes

Another day another event, here's a rear stage pictures, this time with me teaching delegates at a training event for property, This room was filled with advanced students learning the skills to become successful in the business of property investing.

This shows again that I actually do what I say I do, again, another image backing everything I say up and this image again shows virtual clients from around the world. This is one more shot of me at a front end event shows me in a large room speaking to a large audience, The above images show that I walk the walk and don't just talk about it, so whilst building credibility its also shows that I speak in front of large audience and am an animated speaker.

It is imperative that whenever you are on stage whether that be in front of 5 or 500 people that you have someone takes pictures of you in all different angles and positions. If you can also get some video footage as well then that's great as you can use snippets of the video for marketing purposes and teaser clips.

Your marketing should always be around the WOW factor, you need to WOW you audience and show them what is possible, what your message stands for and what you can do to help them get what they want, this is why having a ton of assets in your business is essential.

Let's say you have videographer film your entire session at a speaking engagement then they put together a 1 minute teaser clip or showreel, This is what you would use for your marketing to show the audience that you're someone they want to be around and hear from. Video marketing is powerful and the way forward in my opinion. So you need to build as many videos as possible.

Saying that I don't just limit myself, I would be building an asset bank and this could include

- Videography
- Images of you on stage
- Images of you doing what you teach - Document don't tell them how to
- Testimonials from clients - Written / Video or Social media Postings
- Reviews Sites such as yelp, trust pilot, google reviews
- Social media postings with your brand tagged
- Pictures taken with you and your clients

The list goes on but always be thinking about branding, marketing and how can I use an opportunity to build my asset bank and brand awareness.

Collaborations are a great tool for building awareness to a wider audience of your brand and they have the added benefit of social proof. I would be looking to do as many collaborations with as many people as you can. The power of a collaboration has the ability to make your brand explode over night because of the expert effect, What I mean by this is when you collaborate with an industry leader who let's say has a massive following and is already seen as an authority in the industry then you by default are also seen as someone to listen to because your on their channel or social media.

I've a friend who works in the performance car tuning they own a small workshop which has been doing very well over the last few years, His work is world class and over the years he had been documenting what he has been doings, he's been doing this by constantly pushing his brand and awareness of his work using social media, youtube, and magazine articles.

In the car world if you can get a car that you've worked on and tuned into one of the car magazines then this is massive exposure for you. Alex, the owner was working on an old school mini cooper from the 70's and he done a complete back to bones rebuild on this car.

Alex wanted to use this new project to build his brand and business so he reached out to as many industry specific traders, magazines, bloggers and you tube fanatics that all talk about or have a love for these cars and he invited them all to collaborate on the project with him by assisting with the build and in exchange they all got exposure when the car was finished.

Now the result was that several of them collaborated with Alex on the build, Alex built and awesome car which then went on to feature in the world wide mini magazine and appear on various TV shows. This exploded Alex's business, and he was getting business enquires from literally all over the world which then exploded his car parts business. The other people he collaborated with also got business from it through Alex. This is a great collaboration from Alex and the other partners.

This is just one example, I can think of hundreds of collaborations that work and win for both parties and they should always be in your mind when looking at how to build assets within your business.

Let's look at what you could do to collaborate with someone as a speaker with a message to share. One of the reasons why I speak on stage is to share a message that no matter where you have been in your life this doesn't dictate your future and in particular I'm referring to mental health and depression. I want to spread the word as much as possible that you can get through whatever you're experiencing and to do this I need to reach as many people as possible.

I need to find collaboration partners within the mental health awareness sector that are willing to share a platform with me in order to spread that message so I have reached out to many in order to do this.

It will start small, and for me the collaborations I have done are mainly on instagram with other influencers who also have a similar drive and passion to spread the word about mental health so we have collaborated on their platforms.

So my question to you is who can you collaborate with so you both grow your brand and exposure to help the greater cause?

Write some ideas down now.

-
-
-
-
-
-
-

Whenever considering a collaboration you have to ask your is out a fair collaboration and what will I get from it, Samuel, my property mentor uses this when deciding whether or not he will collaborate with someone

L   LIST
E   EXPERIENCE
A   ASSETS
D   DEALS
S   SATISFACTION

Samuel always asks himself the same questions whenever he enters a collaboration or takes up an invite to speak and he uses the "Leads" system.

Leads System

List

Will this collaboration grow my list of prospects to potential investors or clients.

Experience

Will it be good for experience or will I enjoy the experience, Samuel once flew to South Africa for a 30 minutes speaking engagement purely for the fact it would be a great experience

Assets

Will it be good for capturing assets as described in chapter 6

Deals

Is it likely I could get any business deals from this collaboration

Satisfaction

Finally would it be satisfy to speak or collaborate with someone. Samuel often speaks and works for free in support of his faith and charities purely for the satisfaction of helping and serving others.

Samuel does this for all collaborations and engagements and I suggest you do the same, as a speaker you can very quickly become very busy and your time becomes very valuable so you need to make sure the business and engagements you're taking part in are beneficial to your end goal. You must value what you do and what you offer and at all times hold that value high. One of the reasons why I offer so much value to potential clients for free or very low cost is to give them an opportunity to get to know me.

Chapter 7

Knowledge - Share your Knowledge

The problem I see with a lot of speakers, is they have the knowledge but they lack the skills of delivering that knowledge in a manner that the audience will engage and take in. I'm sure as I have you've sat through a boring lesson or seminar where the speaker relies heavily on an over head projector or slide show and its is just mind numbingly boring and as a result you don't absorb what the speaker has to say.

One of the reasons that I've got so many success students and success stories is because of the way we teach and speak. We call it accelerated learning and what we mean by this is we work and teach in a manner that means the audience is interactive and engaging therefore they retain and learn a lot more that they would by me or you just standing in front of a screen boring them to sleep.

I've even used interaction in this book to get you to do some of the work, and example would be on the last page

So my question to you is who can you collaborate with so you both grow your brand and exposure to help the greater cause?

Write some ideas down now.

I'm getting you to do the work, I as a trainer have asked you a few questions and got you to think about what I want you to think about, in this case who could you collaborate with to help your business?

This get's you thinking and because you are coming up with the answers you're more likely to do it and actually find a partner to collaborate with. If I had just listed all the potential partners there are two issues created instantly,

Firstly; I don't know your specific sector and potential partners and secondly; you know who would be best for your business so if I just list out a load of potential collaboration partners then I'm actually not helping you fully and I will likely miss something out whereas if I ask the right questions and get you thinking and doing the work then my job is done.

This is just one example of sharing the knowledge, in a later chapter i'll be touching on facilitation skills so keep a look out for that as that will take your delivery of the knowledge to the next level.

Now, let's look at a subject that many perceive as complicated therefore has a tendency of becoming boring and as a result your audience may check out of the situation. Now the problem always occurs when you're presenting a complicated or confusing topic, remember a great speaker takes a complicated subject and makes it easy ti understand and implement.

An example I can think of is marketing your business, for many marketing is a minefield and many simply do not know where to start with marketing their business, idea or product so I break it down for them into step by step processes and ill show you this now

I've also done a youtube on marketing which you can find on my youtube channel - Alasdair Cunningham

This is a basic layout of how I would go about speaking about marketing to a room of people looking to learn marketing basics.

M Market
A Add Value
R Reputation
K Know You
E Engaging
T Trust
I Interested
N No Brainer
G Great Service

The great thing about this method is you only have to remember the word marketing and what each letter stands for. Remember earlier when I said you should be an expert of your topic well here's what I mean, If you were to speak about marketing then you don't need notes to present this whole presentation on marketing because you already know it. You only need to remember the words above and your job is to use facilitation and delivery skills to present the above in a great manner.

That one work alone in the right hands could take a whole day of training to deliver, The problem with most people reading this is they are trying to be perfect and overthinking the content, where by I focus massively on the delivery of the content that I'm supposed to be an expert in. The point is if you cannot talk and teach a topic without notes then you quite simply don't know it well enough and you need to brush up on your knowledge of said topic.

Now lets break this "Marketing"

M **Market**

A **Add Value**

R **Reputation**

K **Know You**

E **Engaging**

T **Trust**

I **Interested**

N **No Brainer**

G **Great Service**

Market   2-3 minutes

"First thing in any business is you must understand the market place for your product or service and that means you have to be able to carry out market research effectively" You must know your market as this will help with keeping costs for marketing in control and means any marketing you do is more likely to be effective and get you results.

Think about it, do Nike release a new pair of trainers without understanding its market place and who is their ideal perfect candidate for buying them? Of course not, they'd be absolutely daft if they did. The reason why the big brands sell well is because first they understand their marketplace.

Add Value

Once you understand the market and who is likely to support your business then you can add suitable value to that ideal candidate.

Task - How can we add value to your market place? Write down how you can add value to your market place.

Reputation

2 - 3 minutes

Why is reputation important? Explain why it is and the pitfalls of having a bad reputation and what this will mean for a business.

Interact with the audience ask them how to build a good reputation. Write their answers on the board, this is a great tool to use as a speaker because you're getting the audience to do the work for you.

Know You

4 - 5 minutes including a 2 minutes task

It goes without saying that people will only support your business if they know who you are so that means you have to be a visible in your sector as possible

Go ahead and write down as many ways to make your business or brand more visible so people know you.

Facilitate their answers

Engaging 5 - 6 minutes including 3 minute task and debrief

Again seems obvious but many business actually ignore their clients until they want to sell to them, we need to understand that clients need to know, like and trust you and your brand so that means engagement from us to them on a regular basis so they feel connected to us.

Write down what other benefits does continually engagement with our prospects have?

Facilitate their answers

Trust 3 - 4 minutes including audience share

Trust is big thing in marketing, you need to ensure your marketing material is trustworthy and honest in all aspects, Your ideal prospect will build an opinion of you from day 1 of the first interaction so you need to ensure that the trust factor is always there.

Talk about different ways to build trust.

Interested 5 - 6 minutes including partner share

Keeping your ideal client interested in your brand is essential. How can we do this? Grab a partner and share for 2 minutes

Facilitate

No Brainer 2 - 3 minutes

Now once you understand the marketplace, you've added an immense amount of value, you have built your reputation with them which means they are know who you are and what you stand for because you are in constant engagement with them which means the will build trust because you keep them interested and then you put forward a no brainer of an offer that they simply must buy.

Great Service   2 - 3 minutes

Follow all of the above with great customer service and your set for a very successful marketing campaign and business

What I've just written above if delivered well with the right knowledge and information would go down storm and help many businesses get their heads around marketing. I have incorporated facilitation into the presentation and accelerated learning techniques to get the audience involved and all I would need to remember is the word marketing and what each letter means.

Now if you add the timings up it comes to around 40 minutes, but we haven't factored in your Intro, ETR or WIIFM. When you come to Tell the World we actually put your 45 presentation together with you and you will present this to your group and we help you structure everything so you deliver like a pro, and trust me you will do this confidently and over the course of the program you will realise how great you actually can be.

A lot of people fear that they will run out of content to deliver so what happens is they always overthink the content and write it down word for word and delivery as such, ie; deliver it from notes. We don't allow notes other than a single page of chunking. When you start speaking in the way I will teach you, you will never need to worry about notes or content again.

Remember you are meant to be an expert so you already know you're content, think of it like this, your content is stored in the cloud and your delivery is stored in your mind.

You focus mostly on the delivery and you download the content when you need it. At all times focus on delivering the best presentation without notes to an audience and trust me you will very quickly rise to the ranks of best speaker.

Now the above sessions on marketing could be done over 1 day or 2 days if you choose, however the longer the session and event would obviously dictate further facilitation and tasks so the audience are getting value from it.

Whether you follow this method of simplifying your knowledge or not doesn't matter, the principles are the same, you must make your subject simple to understand and easy to follow. Remember as a speaker and a leader the people who want to listen to you want you to be the gap between where they are and where you are or where they want to be, the only way to do this is to take great content and help them process it easier by making it as simple as possible.

Anyone can make something sound difficult and quite often they will because the fear others will copy or do better than them, often the rich don't like to reveal their "inner secrets" to wealth because they want to appear smarter than you when in fact that's not often the case. For me a great leader is also a great speaker and a great leader is someone who creates other leaders and shares their knowledge with open arms to help and inspire the masses and if one of your students gets better at than you then surely as a great leader that is the best testimonial ever for your teachings.

I believe in teaching and inspiring to the best of my ability and giving everything I have, when I leave a stage I guarantee you that there is nothing I don't share or give back. A good speaker is an open book with their knowledge and I would be vary of any speaker who is continually holding things back from you.

When it comes to selling your knowledge and skill sets through training then obviously you aren't going to give everyone the same amount of information because people are obviously paying you for your advanced information and teachings but at every level of event whether that's a free entry level or a £5000 advanced program whatever you say you're going to give them always ensure you do.

It's very easy in the early days to try and do to much for people for free because your trying to build your brand and business but you must protect what you offer and not give it away for free, now I'm not saying don't do anything for free at all what I'm saying is value your skill set as a speaker and hold that value high and get paid your worth.

Let me explain that a little, earlier I referred to Samuel's "leads" system and we use this when assessing an interaction with a potential client or collaboration partner. Now as your popularity grows so will the requests you get from people asking for help, asking for a coffee, to meet for dinner etc and you need to be careful of this and let me tell you why.

If I took every offer to meet someone I'd never get anything done for a start but more importantly the person asking to meet you doesn't bring any value to the table, the purely want to meet you to discuss business and learn from you for free and there is no fair exchange. I can buy my own coffee thank!

The reason I have so much free of low cost value is partly for this problem, you see when I get such requests I simply respond with a polite message offering them the opportunity to attend my Six Figure Speaker Summit event, or grab a copy of one of my books or watch a podcast, that way they are getting what they want within reason and I'm strengthening my position as an authority within the space.

Your time will become very valuable and you must protect that and only allow people into your space who value it the same as you do and trust me there are plenty of people who will value your skill set and time the way you do, I know this because I often get paid £1000's from people to attend programs with me and to have the opportunity to hear what I have to say. I'm currently writing this chapter in a hotel room, where I'm the lead trainer at a two day event starting tomorrow morning where delegates have traveled to learn some advanced property strategies.

People will value your expertise and pay you handsomely to learn from you once you realise your worth and know you can deliver that message effectively to impact change in someone else's life. Remember that earlier on in this book we discussed building assets within your business and brand and your knowledge is probably the biggest asset you have so to give that away for free is frankly ridiculous.

Over the years I've spent a small fortune in learning from the best mentors from around the world, literally I've flown half way across the globe to learn from the best teachers, guru's and leaders and if I were to add the total amount up its getting on for £60,000 in training and mentoring and I continually do whatever it takes to expand my knowledge bank.

I attended a training program in Chennai, India and this is where I learned so many skills but mainly I learned the skill of stage craft and delivery and how to be an effective leader. Over the week long intensive program which is limited to just a handful of people per year I was pushed to step out of my comfort zone so far I couldn't even see it, If I told you some to the task I had to complete you would never believe me because it is out of context but they do this for the same reason I will push you. It will force you to change something that impacts your life. During this particular event I went from the lowest of lows to the highest peaks over the week long program and trust me I needed it.

At Tell the World I do the same with my students, I push them and push them to step out of their comfort zone, and when they think they are out I push them some more and the reason is because I know that most of you reading this live in your comfort zone and that's not working for you and if you're to grow and develop then that's isn't going to happen whilst your in your comfort zone. Remember great speakers are also great leaders and that means lead don't follow, your job is to pave the way for those who need your knowledge and help and my job as a trainer is to help you become a world class trainer, speaker and facilitator so you can impact change on your audience whoever that may be but it all starts with you

Chapter 8

Enjoy - Make it Fun

Ask yourself when you enjoy what you're doing are you more likely to absorb and take in the information?

There is two parts to this chapter and I want to emphasis these and ensure you enjoy what you do. The last thing you want to do is burn out and resent what you do so make it fun. The reason why I can travel the country, stay in hotels, share my message to the masses is because I truly love what I do. I do not see what I do as a job or work, for me it's 100% about my passion for helping, serving and working with people to impact change. As corny as this sounds its really not about the money as I know the value I deliver to people will result in me getting paid very well.

As I said money should never be the main focus point nor should you ever put money on a pedestal and that being said you should always focus on the mission and value first. Listen when you truly care about people and their journey and their story you build connection with them and they become your fuel to keep going. You whether you like it or now become a part of their life, I've built many great friendships with former and current students and trust me we have a lot of fun in the process of teaching and inspiring people. As I said the money is a by-product of the service and value you bring to the audience.

Now stats show that when you make learning more fun you retain 80% information and you remember the information for a longer period of time. I'm sure you can think of lessons you took from games and tasks you done when you were at school or in your earlier days Of course you will and this is exactly why we incorporate learning with fun and games,

You need your audience to enjoy what you teach so they stay with you.

Throughout teaching there are commonly two types of way to learn

Passive and Active learning

Active Learning

Active learning is where the students participate in learning that requires activities, discussions and tasks and this has many benefits. The method of active learning enforces learning and creates different perspectives, opinions and understandings. When students interact with each other in active learning tasks they tend to retain the information a lot more and that means the results are going to be much better.

Examples of Active Learning

- Partner Share
- Group Shares
- Grab a partner and discuss
- Games
- Tasks
- Group exercises
- Basically anything that requires the audience to get out of their seats and get hands on.

Now if you've attended any of my events you will for sure have taken part in active learning, I do this all the time and the reasons are very much proven.

Think about it, let's say I'm running an event all about public speaking and I have an audience who mostly new or never does any speaking on stage.

I ask the question what makes a great public speaker?

Now ask yourself, would you learn more if I simply write down and tell you what the answers are? Or would you learn more if I put you into a partner exercise and asked you to tell me what you think makes great speaker?
I'm sure you'd answer with the latter and of course you would learn more if I make the whole situation fun and interactive.

You got to remember that your a trainer and facilitator and that means you must facilitate and understand that the excellence is already with your delegates, what I mean by that is often they know the answers and what they need to do but they don't do it or know they know the answers.

Your job is to make learning fun and interactive and force the information out of them by using facilitation and your skills to ensure the environment and context is safe and fun so they can excel. Whenever you put the audience into tasks it forces them to work and think and that means that they will find the answers within themselves.

Another way to keep your delegates actively learning is to incorporate games within learning and let me share a game I do at a property event to give you inspiration as to what games you can put into your learning.

It's called Ball Pits

I do this game at a program called buy refurb refinance which is a program I teach as part of the property investors academy where we teach people how to find, refurb and refinance a house to withdraw their initial investment therefore having a no money left in property deal. This in itself can be a complicated theory to explain to people as they often struggle to understand that aspect of recycling you're cash with this strategy. What I mean by that is you can recycle the same pot of cash to buy multiple properties if done correctly.

The way the game works is as follows

Each ball has a value

Green ball	1 point
Blue ball	1 point
Pink ball	0 points
Yellow ball	2 points

We set the room up so at one side of the room are ball pits with a pictures of ball colours in there, note - there are fewer yellow balls than anything else.

At the other side of the room are boxes and the purpose of the game is each team has 2 minutes to get as many points by adding the balls to your teams box.

In a nutshell each team has to transport a ball of any colour to the box and after the 3 minutes I go around and add up all the points in the box. Team with most points win.

The lesson here is that a yellow ball is worth 2 points however there is only a few yellow balls in each ball pit therefore I'm forcing the teams to think how can they use the few yellow balls to maximise points.

The answer is in the rules that each player gets giving. There is no rule saying that the balls has to stay in the box. The clever players realise that they can put the ball in, take the ball out then put it back in ie recycle the ball within the box, the yellow ball is their money, they put their money into a deal then recycle.

Once you play this game and understand property it just seems to click for some people, the game serves to help people click with the concept of recycling your cash and also takes at least 1 hour to facilitate so keeps you delegates active, on their feet and having fun.

Passive learning

Is the type of teaching commonly seen in schools and conventional education where the information may be presented in the form of lectures and readings. In any case, the student is accountable for paying attention, asking questions, and performing well on tests.

Passive learning promotes defining, describing, listening, and writing skills. This process initiates convergent thinking, where a given question typically has only one right answer. We rarely teach passively as we know that the learning is far better received when taught actively.

I hope form reading above you incorporate fun, games, tasks and interaction into any presentation you make but please do think about any games or tasks you do carefully as they need to have an outcome. You must know what the outcome is and understand how the game is going to help the delegates get to that outcome. So plan the games and tasks thoroughly.

We also focus a lot on energy at events and we want our audience to be in a high energy state, we teach this as we need people to be high energy and ready to take action and be alert, now we don't do this to create a party type environment, we do this because energy is literally everything. Everything we do we must do with energy, let me explain.

We all have that friend that no matter what we do, what we say and what opportunities we present will down play the situation, they will suck the life out of you and whatever you bring to the table. I know you know the person I'm talking about and we all have that person in our life

Likewise, we also have a person that is high energy, positive, encouraging and always pushed you forward and we all have that person in your life.

Now, if I asked your friends which one of the above you are. How would they answer? How do they perceive you to be?

High energy or low energy?

If its low energy then it's unlikely that they or anyone will do business with you ever so if you're looking to do business which involves people then you better lift the energy and be seen as a high energy person.

Remember your job as a speaker is to keep the energy high, the delegates alert, interactive, awake, having fun and most importantly learning skills that they retain and will impact them and others they know, and we do this by teaching in an active manner whilst incorporating games, tasks, and interaction.

When you come along to the Six figure speakers summit you will see I keep you all busy throughout the day and ask you to interact with strangers, work in groups, converse and work with people from all backgrounds and I do this because I know that you are likely to do business with some of these people and ultimately see a different perspective from a different view point and that's how you have fun while learning and jeep your delegates coming back over and over.

Chapter 9

Refreshing - Breakthrough Content

We live in the era of information overload and everywhere you look there is literally masses of information available readily at people's fingertips, every man and his dog are uploading information for people in order to grow their following. Whilst I'm all for this I'm also vary of it because there is so much misinformation out there and I think it comes down to people spreading the information without the credentials to spread the information, we spoke about this in a earlier chapter about those teaching and spreading information with-out the credibility, experience or knowledge to know what they are saying is correct.

In this chapter I'll be explaining how you can keep your content refreshing and unique so people want to hear what you have to say. I mean it doesn't take a genus to work out that if you can make your content entertaining and deliver it well then you will also be known for refreshing content but all to often people just repeat content and don't even attempt to put their own style into it.

Let me give you a working example to help you understand this better and for this we are going to use public speaking as the topic.

Now there is a lot of information out in the worldwide web about public speaking and presenting and the basic of public speaking are the same regardless of where you learn about.

- Find your topic
- Master your Topic
- Prepare a presentation
- Deliver presentation

- Receive feedback
- Improve
- Repeat

It's not rocket science and if you wanted to you could easily learn how to public speak from this book or online but what makes my content unique and refreshing? Ask yourself? Just think about that for a minute, what makes my content differ from others?

I can tell you that my content has the same basic format as most other speaker trainers and teachings however I've added various elements to the training that make it unique and refreshing.

How and what have I done to do this?

Let me explain, this whole book is based around a system, a unique and branded system that you've never seen or heard of until you read this book.

The system is known as the Six Figure Speaker System and this whole book is based on that system. The system works

and is my step by step process for putting together a presentation and being able to deliver that presentation in style so people learn from you. I do this with many presentations and as a result the delegates learn considerably more as they don't have to focus on boring long lessons from passive teachers who have no skills for presenting.

When you put your topic into a system it goes from being just words on a page to a workable achievable easy to follow process. This is has the benefit of branding and trademarking your business assets which means nobody will copy what you do and if they do you have copyright and can enforce action against it.

Remember your job as a speaker and leader is to present information in an easy to follow and implement system which can be easily understood. People remember systems and will share your system which means your followers will promote your brand.

I could do this for any content and make it refreshing, Let me share another example of building an investors database for your property business. I teach a lot of property courses as I've done considerably well in property and love to share this knowledge with those looking to make money in the sector and one of the key issues people raise is being able to raise finance, find investors and find joint venture opportunities so I put together a system for finding investors.

Now I could easily just use a projector and play slides after slide on

- Networking
- Positioning yourself
- Conversation topics
- Pitching

- Negotiation
- Finding investors

And I'm sure that would be good and adequate but I'm not looking for adequate, I'm looking for world class training and sessions and to do this you must make your content refreshing, unique and new and the best way to do this is to put the topics above into a system or process that is easily replicated and remembered, so here's what I came up with

I	IDENTIFY
N	NETWORK
V	VALUE
E	ENGAGING
S	SOCIAL MEDIA
T	TELL THE WORLD
O	OFFER
R	REPUTATION

I then cover each session in detail and utilise facilitation skills to get the audience to understand the process even better, Facilitation is what makes an average speaker become a world class speaker. Facilitation is the skill of facilitating the audience, drawing out the excellence and often being the facilitator between the audience members and this requires the skill to listen and ask questions that provokes learning or further questions.

Often with these questions you can get a member of the audience to reflect not so much on the here and now; but often the what have I missed out on by not doing it this way? The use of questions is crucial and after every exercise we have a debrief, your debrief can consist of multiple smaller exercises and these could but are not limited to

- Individual task
- Group Task

- Partner Share
- Group Share

So let's say I was teaching the session on Identify, I would first explain what I mean by identify. I would utilise all the tools I have to hand to emphasis the teachings and that could be anything on my stage. After explain what I mean by Identify I could then set them to a task.

For instance; the task I set them is to go off an look at who they ideal investors would be and start to identify them - I instruct them to be specific about demographic, salary levels, hobbies, work patterns, careers and many other factors that would allow them to identify their perfect investor. I would allow them 5-15 minutes to do this task depending on how long my overall presentation.

Once everyone is back in their seats I would then facilitate the task.

[partner share]

Grab your self a partner and share with them what you learned about your ideal investor? Give them 2 minutes each partner.

[group share]

After this I would ask who would like to share to the whole room?

I would then ask a few questions such as

"What happened?"

"What did you learn?"

"What are you going to do differently going forward?"

These questions will lead to other questions, and I would ask maybe 2 or 3 audience member to do a group share before I moved on. The reason why I do a group share followed by facilitation is because often you will learn things from those sharing what they learned from the exercise. This whole session could take 10 - 20 minutes or even longer if I wanted to add to facilitation exercises.

I would then move onto the next word, but before I reveal the next word I would "salt" the word before revealing it, now what this means is I'm building anticipation to what the word is to keep the audience engaged, and when I reveal the word they are alert and ready for it.

An example of salting

"I've just revealed to you the importance of identifying your investors, now we know this we can proceed to the next word and if you don't do this next step you are literally just wasting your time, I mean it will be pointless in identifying who you're looking for, its essential that if you want to position yourself in front of your ideal investor then you must do this, the next step is ...."

Then I would reveal the word "Networking"

I would then as before explain networking, the best ways to network and meet people, I would talk about what not to do and the common failures within networking.

The first task I would do would be to get the delegates to write down all the places that they could network to find their ideal investor.

[group share]

Who would like to share what they wrote down?

Next I would then ask the question, How many of you would give your 20 second pitch at a networking event if given the opportunity?

Next task would be to get into pairs and for the next 10 minutes you need to prepare your 20 second pitch that you would say when you get the opportunity. I would then get them helping each other to prepare their pitch. After 10 minutes I would then facilitate again

[partner share]

You're each going to have 5 minutes to present your pitch to the other partner, now I know its only meant to be a 20 second pitch but you can do it, then repeat it until you get it good and so it flows freely without stuttering or you waffling.

[group share]

Who would like to share their 20 second pitch? I would invite some volunteers to then present their pitch and I would then facilitate them and give the coaching on a 121 level however at all times keeping the audience involved and interacted, and the process continues throughout all of the other letters in the system.

I continually facilitate and interact with the audience to keep them engaged, learning and understanding the teachings, I also use state changes to get keep the audience engaged and alert, a state change is an interaction or action that changes your state.

For instance;

- Audience call backs
- Fill in the gaps
- Repeat a word
- Asking for interaction ie Raise a hand
- Turn to a neighbour and give them a high five
- Stand up
- Stretch
- Jumping jacks
- The list goes on

The brain can only focus for about 20 minutes so as a trainer and speaker we need to do a state change when we feel the audience is drifting off or not fully focussed on the teachings and the type of state change you would use is very much dependant on the type of audience, You wouldn't do a high five state change if you're presenting to a board of directors as that would be awkward but you may do a high five state change to a room of high energy people learning about business. You must judge the room and the audience to determine what's appropriate, needed and expected from your audience.

[audience call back]

This is where I would ask them to call back the answer to an open question

[fill in the gaps]

This is where I would ask the audience to fill in the gaps of a sentence of phrase that is key to learning, for instance here's a very basic example but you could make these about your specific topic and it will enhance learning.

"Let's go to the _____ to watch a movie?"

[repeat a word]

This is where I asked for a call back to repeat an important work or phrase, lets show you an example

"Over the last few years, I've spent thousands learning how to generate income through business and I found that the best way was by investing"

"What's the word please?"

I told them that investing was what I found to be the best way so all I asked them to do is repeat the word, ie investing. This reinforced the learning that investing was the best for me. Its a very simple example but you get my point.

[Asking for interaction ie raise your hand]

Very simple state change here and used frequently to ask for interaction and make sure that the audience members are understanding what you have just said. For instance; If I just done a teaching and it's complicated I would say something along the lines of does everyone understand this, raise your hand and say yes.You can use the hand raise to get many interactions and acknowledgement, Whenever you ask for interaction in any way you must thank the audience as they this is the polite thing to do an keeps you audience interacting. If you never thanked them, they would slowly stop interacting.

I'm not going to explain every interaction and state change as it is pretty much common sense. Just remember to mix it up a little and do state changes regularly to keep you audience engaged and interacting. You also as a great speaker want to keep the whole audience involved and listening and you need to ensure that even the people at the back of the room are involved. You can do this easily with eye contact and walking through the audience if this is possible.

When you add in the tips from this chapter and others you have the knowledge to put together a presentation and deliver it well, now you need to hone and develop if you want to get to six figure speaker status. You can come along and spend a few days with me to hone and develop these skills at my event called The Six Figure Speaker Summit. You can come along for just £1.

- You will the learn the '7 Step Speaker System' so that you can - Speak confidently to groups of 5 - 500
- Learn how to GET Paid Six-Figures doing what you love - Turn your passion into profit
- Present without the use of notes and never forget what your going to say
- Gain confidence and overcome your fears
- Become a leader and inspire others - and much more

You can get all the info you need by checking out our website

www.6figurespeaker.com

Chapter 10

What Others Say about the Author

Here's a few written testimonials off current and past students that I've worked with, I'm showing you these because these are just normal working people like you and I and they found themselves in a rut and needed something to help them out of it and they found it my training. Take a read yourself and make your own mind up

Joe Nicol

Alasdair is one of the best men I have been lucky enough to know. He cares deeply about people and wants to see you succeed. He has been a huge support to me over these two years and it's an honour to share a few words for him.
To set the context I was 6 months into my property training. Alasdair ran zoom calls every week where 20 of us would share our wins and challenges we were facing. On this particular week, I had lost my job. I was frustrated and spoke aloud and said '

'It's not possible like you say, it's not as easy as you make out and people can't make money as they did before"

Alasdair questioned my belief system. He asked if I believed in myself and the training. I admitted that I did not and felt property was unrealistic for me.

Alasdair said

''Listen, you book viewings, and I will take a day off for free and drive to your area and join you for the day. I will show you that this is possible!"

I didn't really speak or know Alasdair at this time, and my sceptical mind thought the only reason he is doing this is to make money. We met two weeks later after he drove 6 hours and the first thing he said was "I have not come here to make any money, I will give you my investors to keep, and help you sell it, I don't want any of it, I have only come to show you that it's possible and you can do this" I made £3000 that day and he did not take a penny. For me this showed his true character.

He taught me that it is possible and gave me the energy to speak to agents and landlords to get them on your side. It was a massive eye-opener and I copy the same skills today.

Alasdair has the ability to break people down and then build them back up stronger and he did this to me at one of his events. He broke me and created an environment where I found the courage to tell him things from my past that I have not said to anyone in my whole life. He never once judged me and understood firsthand about mental health. He put me in touch with the right people for help and has continued to support me to this day. I really do not believe I would have spoken to anyone if it were not for him and I am more grateful for this than anything.

Alasdair thank-you from the bottom of my heart for all the time, love and belief you have given to me. You encourage men to be themselves unapologetically. My family have noticed a huge change in my mindset and I am not the same person directly because of you. Whenever I face my fears, you are always in my mind. You are a hero of mine and you will never fully understand the impact you have created for me and my family's future.

Massive love, loyalty, and respect always.

Jamie Higgs

I've been asked to deliver the eulogy which I would have declined had I not had the Tell The World training. Looking back across the last few years and the different events I attended I can honestly say the energy and focus you and the team brought to the table was second to none. The content was spot on, the feedback was brutal at times but I like that because you slice through layers of bullshit in an instant.

Whenever I've asked for help or feedback you have delivered that in a professional direct manner (cutting through the bullshit). Your direct, honest (sometimes not what people want to hear but need to hear) approach has influenced the way in which I conduct myself within the property world, be kind, professional but don't tolerate BS.

I admire your loyalty to your clients, you give 100% all the time and leave nothing in the tank at every event I've been to.

Tell the world was a game-changer for me, I thought I could talk to crowds of people but that was just reading from a piece of paper. I now know I can flick a switch and deliver content rather than recite information. As I said above I would have declined the offer to read my friend's eulogy because I wouldn't have done it justice, now I can flick a switch and tap into emotions in a way that won't stop/affect the delivery.

On top of that, the process you go through during those 3 - 4 days opens up parts of the mind which I didn't think could be tapped into and exposes who you/we really are, strengths, weaknesses warts and all, but in a safe environment.

A few messages/visions are tattooed in my mind which helps when the little voice kicks in. "I am the Voice" is one. When I visited your Bedford project, I did pick up property-related tips but the one thing that stuck with me is when you did the video, and how you coped when it went wrong. My friend 'Kris' who was with me at the time is in the music/performing industry side of things and pointed out how professional you were on camera, again flicking the switch. You are a leading figure in the property world and I wish you every success.

Giulia Grizzardi

TTW is an intense and genuine program. It can only serve you if you are ready to play full out in all aspects. If you let yourself be guided by the incredible Alasdair, listening and intensely absorbing all the steps of the program, you will have the opportunity to discover a part of yourself never heard and seen before.

I was very sceptical doing this course, I am not a person who can look inside and believe I can change. I managed to dig deep inside myself, a bottom that I did not know I had, but which then, albeit with a lot of effort, I managed to climb, just like an uphill wave. As of today, after TTW, I feel unstoppable, strong, genuine, and full of power(what ever you class as power)a power that I had kept suppressed and lying, but which is now a beautiful discovery.

All this and much more, thanks to you Alasdair, thanks to your ability to read people up to their soul, thanks to your hand always there to grab us and never gave up on me, thanks to your tenacity to give me the strength to continue even when the emotions have taken over big time.

This is a program that I hope will be extended and deepened, because few people have the ability to express the greatness of the soul through the medium "voice" and few people are truly leaders, but you absolutely have this ability, and I'm looking forward to see what will come next, as I'll be there!

Prity Chauhan

Alasdair is a truly inspirational speaker, mentor & coach.
He is authentic & delivers with conviction. I attended the Tell The World training, which I can say was one of the best training courses I have ever attended. Alasdair delivered the training with passion & although I felt uncomfortable at times throughout the training, I felt bold enough to take part in activities that I never thought I would, as a result of Alasdair's guidance and support

The way I conduct myself & speak with confidence now, is as a result of this fantastic training, delivered by a world class coach.

Sarah White

Hi Alasdair

I am happy to say that since I met you on the Business of Property Investing course and subsequent Tell the World my own personal development has been extensive.

Since then I've been so much more positive I've had a morning routine, hit my weight goal and in the middle of smashing several personal goals.

Tell the World was life changing I've gained so much confidence my life now has purpose and I've taken complete control of my life. Since last weeks sales training our revenue has significantly increased and a big pay rise is on the cards! to summarise we have made great progress in the Will writing business.

My property portfolio is growing and I've also started a building company to do the refurb for my BRRRs in partnership with Chris uncle. Wow now I've written this out it's mad how much I've achieved! Thank you

Chapter 11

Exact Next Steps

Okay so hopefully you've enjoyed this book, either way I hope you have found this nook helpful to your business and brand and If I can help you please reach out to ask for help.

Review   I would really appreciate an honest review. Amazon would be best for this.

Share   If you've enjoyed the book and you know someone who would benefit from this please share it with them.

Social Media   Tag me in your pictures on socials - I love seeing people benefit from my teachings, I often will share your picture

If you want to meet me and go over the Six Figure Speaker System in person you are invited to join me for a live event, The Six Figure Speaker Summit is not to be missed and you can attend for just £1.

You can register for the next event by scanning the QR come below

You can book Alasdair for any Speaking Engagements by emailing hello@Alasdair-Cunningham.com

Please share our message and all our social media pages.

 www.6figurespeaker.com

www.alasdair-cunningham.com

 https://www.instagram.com/
alasdair_cunningham/

 https://www.facebook.com/
alasdair.cunningham